The Quotient of My Self
Divided by Myself

The Quotient
of My Self
Divided

Miles A. Coon

by Myself

Press 53

Winston-Salem

Press 53, LLC
PO Box 30314
Winston-Salem, NC 27130

First Edition

Cover art, "Two Sides of the Story," oil on canvas,
Copyright © 1992 by Felix Sherman.
Used with permission of the artist.

Cover dsign by Claire V. Foxx

Author Photo by Jacek Gancarz

Library of Congress Control Number
2022938864

ISBN 978-1-950413-52-2

Dedicated to Mimi
who dedicates her life to my happiness—
to my son, Matthew,
my daughter, Jennifer,
to my grandson, Elias
and to my beloved teachers,
Thomas Lux, Laure-Anne Bosselaar,
Billy Collins, Vijay Seshadri,
Stephen Dobyns, Marie Howe.
Special thanks to Nickole Brown
and Jessica Jacobs who helped
deliver every page of this collection.

Acknowledgments

The author thanks the editors of the publications where these poems first appeared, occasionally in different form:

Lumina, "Groomed" & "You Draw Me"

Rattapallax, "Childhood Scene"

Never Before: Poems About First Experiences, Four Way Books, 2005, edited by Laure-Anne Bosselaar, "Trade Show"

The chapbook *Homeland Security* (Jeanne Duval Editions, 2006), "Childhood Scene," "The Shrine," "Speechless," "Witness," "Trade Show," "A Man," "The Swimming Pool," "For My Father," "Groomed," "Intersection," "West Nile Virus," "Condolence Call," "New York, September 2001," "Trespass," "Wild Kingdom," "You Draw Me," & "We Go to Bed Again"

Contents

III. Leading Man

We make out of the quarrel with others, rhetoric,
but of the quarrel with ourselves, poetry.
                    —William Butler Yeats

More than the Sum of My Parts

I failed at my first speaking part: dutiful son
at the dinner table. I forgot my lines.

In the schoolyard, I tried out for victim:
bullied, thrown to the ground.
My crybaby was sheer perfection.

In the classroom, I used my compass and my rule
to become a star, I wrote the loner's script, then
the clown full of pathos and quips.

Then Virginia gentleman with a flask in college, philosopher
complete with pipe, explorer of my own body,
authentic groans.

Three-piece lawyer's suit, pocket watch, I
delivered arguments from both sides
of my mouth. I loved government-lawyer,
the big credentials, a cog in the vast machinery
of the federal bureaucracy.

My longest run was as the son in the father-son
family business. Those years as the long-suffering,
second-guessed, were my best, I guess. But when
the leading man left the scene, I could not hide
my grief.

Wandering the pasture, I used a field guide
to explore the natural world. I dressed in poet's black,
sipped Chablis, spilled my guts
in un-free verse. I learned to lean forward
with intensity around a table. I recited
Wordsworth and Yeats, railed
against the ravages of corporate greed.

I, as cameo husband and father, walked on
to thunderous applause. When my hearing went,
I played it well. *Come closer, speak up. I won't
live forever.*

I. Obedient Son

The entrance

of my parents' small apartment
was a backlit, blue-mirrored bar,
with their friends fixed
by gravity to swivel stools camouflaged
in Palomino skins. They spun there
to rhumba music, the blue nude
askew on the wall; mother's laughter,
ice-cubes cracking glass.
Outside that room, World War II;
Brooklyn blacked-out.
Not a peep out of you, father said
and closed my bedroom door.

New Year's Eve, 1944

Early evening: They are about to leave me,
age six, before the babysitter came.
In the street, air raid wardens
shout and blow their whistles. Mother
tells my forehead not to worry,
but she's not wearing a skirt, just
a sequined blouse, her legs all exposed,
and father, in half a rented tuxedo—no pants.
Stop! I yell, *you can't go out like that.*
Out the door they go.
The elevator takes them away. Two minutes,
they're back. They shout, *Happy New Year!*
I stand there before them, enraged.
Oh, sweetie, mother says,
we were only joking.

I still refer to them as others
refer to the sky,
to navigate. Like shining stars,
lost in daytime. Only at night
did they reveal themselves—
nomads, beautiful at a distance.

Speechless

After Robert Lowell

Squat pinch-bottled soldiers,
one killed each day at dusk—
Scotch behind the bar
is what my father lived for.
Stashed, emptied, restocked
like a river.

Mother served him hors d'oeuvres
on a silver tray,
leashed to a collar,
one notch too tight to speak.

Father stood, helmet-hard.
When he dropped
his jacket, I ran
to pick it up. *Leave it!*
I want your mother
to walk all over it.

Lies

What makes you
you
is the small machine
inside
that never quits
asking questions.

You are
a small boy
in a bath
and in the sky
a billion stars
are watching.

The small machine
and a billion stars
know I lie.

I ask, *What's that?*
pointing to a rose
on the flagstone wall.

Look it up.

Father says, *The earth revolves around my penis,*
Teacher says, *The earth revolves around the sun.*

Does the earth revolve around Father's penis?
It does, Mother says, *in a way.*

In the loam of all I know
but don't know I know
I dig.

Sign in the Window

"Boy Wanted!"

For what? I asked
from the backseat of the Nash Rambler.

For cooking, father said.
*That's where they stuff
little boys, one at a time,
into the mouth of a big machine—*

Bam! he shouted,
*A Boy Burger
comes out the other end,
raw, bloody, and ready to eat.*

I told them, *I will throw my glasses
into the grinder
if you ever come for me.*

Our Blue Merle Collie

On the leash, he strained,
pulling me down Stuart Street
toward the vacant lot on Henry
where tall grasses grew undisturbed
and maple trees were rioting,
unable to contain themselves.

We called him Blue Boy.
Born to shepherd bleating flocks,
ears cocked for strays, sharp-eyed
for the peripheries, he was cold-nosed,
thundered his deep-throated bark.

When he peed, modest, he turned
his tail away from me. I was afraid
his tug would pull the ground
out from under me. Afraid
I couldn't hold him,
without a chance of keeping up,
I wound his leather leash twice
around my wrists. And then,

flat out, Blue Boy, a streak—
and me, dragged on my belly,
my knees skinned, skimming his world.
My shoulder socket popped, trying to stop.

I did not let go until my father,
in his Cadillac, cut Blue Boy off.
How he barked, that dog, so happy
to see him. My father, too, leaping
from the car, ignoring my bloody self,
my weeping in pain.

Then, the crack of father's fists on Blue Boy's back.

He hurled me into the back seat,
walked around the car, tied
Blue Boy's leash to the back bumper.
He made him run, both of us whimpering.
He made him keep up
with three hundred and eighty-five horses.

Breakfast

Pancakes puckered and tanned in the frying pan.
Mother, at the stove, her back to me
in the winter kitchen, two places set
on a table scarred and splintered, a leg lost
the night before. I saw the orange juice slanted
in the glasses, Aunt Jemima beaming from her leaning
bottle, Mother's swollen cheek, the sunglasses
that kept her blackened eyes from speaking.
She passed a stack without a word. We ate
with care at the battered table, a bruised silence,
as if averted eyes and swallowed words
could change our history, our future. I cleared
the dirty dishes. She cautioned me to *shhhh*,
as we froze there, listening, to Father's step
on the stairs. How the wind caroused and howled.
How the snow began to cover our plot.

Jocko

Button-eyed monkey
who warms my bed in winter,
nose to nose, we two.

We wake in shadows
cast by black wrought-iron bars—
my welded window.

Tall cold glass of milk,
Aunt Sophie's chocolate cake, snow.
No one cares but us.

Cry Uncle

I kept my breathing slow,
posing as a child in sleep,
blankets up to my ears.

Father's dusty, musty
earthy smell, made my shoulders shake.
Did you lose your socks? he asked, holding

my sock to his nose, falling, arms
outstretched, to the floor. I put on
my glasses, dove from the bed

on top of him—a heap, father and son.
What's going on in here? Mother straddled
the sharp edge of her voice.

I socked him, father said,
and the little twerp socked me back.
Then he tickled me until I cried.

At the Table

I dine on the disappointment
in his eyes. Is it my shoelace,
left untied, or my uncertainty
he can't abide? Was it my curt hello
yesterday before we sat
that angers him today?

I've watched him
tear towns, cities, entire counties
apart with his bare hands.
Furious father, he never left me alone.
I saw him rip thick phone books
in two—he tore me, too, then,
in half.

An Eye for an Eye

I had an eye
for an eye, the one
that turned in
(let's call it his cross
eye), and an ear
for trouble
on the domestic front,
even then, age ten,
lost to books
in the public library,
due home by five,
arrive at seven
in the winter dark,
mother's car gone,
father's, hot-hooded,
in the garage. Not good,
the booze in him
since five, the kitchen
chair lying on its side
when I arrive on tiptoe
peeking in from the mud-
room among the hung,
still-cold coats. I knew
the commandment
of fallen furniture:
Thou shalt not move.
So I hung there,
shivering on a hook,
as my fearful bladder
filled, then let go.
That urine soaked
my shoes and socks,
so I unraveled
the rank laces, squatting
like a girl, peeled
the reeking wool

from my frozen feet,
and crawled into
the bright fluorescent
light, my knees leaving
streaks on the scrubbed
linoleum. I felt
his footsteps in the floor.

He found me curled
like an aborted fetus
in his path,
and he recoiled:
Where the fuck
have you been?
It's after seven.
And then he saw,
his cross eye turning in,
my urine, the unspeakable
traces of my shame.
You've pissed your pants,
he hollered, then laughed.
Be a man, goddammit,
be a man. Then his hands
pulled down my pants.
He made me wash
my dirty shorts right there
while he made himself
another drink.
When mother entered,
I was bare-assed
at the kitchen sink.
She covered me
in her raccoon coat
still full of her body warmth.
She and I left him then
to change.

When I Was a Boy

I wasn't allowed to make a scene.
Poor me worked like a charm.

So did, *I couldn't help it*, and,
But I tried my best.

I was too numb for knives.

Eventually, I made a scene
in a shoebox, cut a square hole in one end
to look into the world created on the floor,
ceiling, surrounding walls. Light was
my problem, so I slid the lid just enough
to see the scene in dim confinement.
I painted black-limbed trees
against a white, cloudless sky, the trunks
lined up like kids waiting for the bus.
Below the crisscrossed branches, I stuck
a clay figure, looking up. When I
peered in, I saw myself
staring at the world. I never knew
what others felt, seeing that boxed-in boy,
underneath bare trees, an empty sky.

Birthday Fool

The candles come as no surprise
but the party does.
Bob, the bully, the athlete, Dave,
the other zitless kids scrubbed,
sitting to my right and left,
and I am four-eyed at the head
of the table. What's their agenda
here? And these gifts bestowed
as if they owe me
for the lonely walks to school.
I'm no fool, but today
I'm fooled by their careful smiles,
the Hallmark cards inscribed
To a Great Guy,
To a Swell Friend.
At twelve, I'm on the brink
of a precipice. Quite a big word
for a boy my size: words
are my fists, my gifts,
the stuff of lies like layer-cake,
all the saccharine birthday refrains.

The Country

In the distance, stick shift and rumble seat,
the hiss from my father's lips passing
for a laugh, a Sunday drive, soldiers
back from the big war, hitchhike
in their uniforms, 1946. Mother throws
them kisses, waves, all those brave boys,
their duffle bags beside them like sleeping
heaps of dreams, on the side of the road.
I knew nothing of the bomb, other
than a picture in *Life* of a mushroom
cloud and its vast unfurling. The news
took so long to reach us, radios slow
to warm up, their thin signals, songs
etched in memory, images pressed in tin,
Mother and Father singing, *They asked me*
if I knew our true love was true,
and I, from the back seat, *I, then of course*
replied, when a sleeping flame dies, smoke
gets in your eyes. Just once, all of us together
singing, driving east toward the country
and the sun, away from Brooklyn, to the house
that would become our home, four flowering
Linden trees, a sunken garden, and so many roses—
American Beauties climbing
the flagstone walls.

Kings Point, Long Island

Our new rooms are groomed
by servants who, like family,
are sworn to secrecy.
Mother peeks
through windows
as his car pulls up,
listening to the sound
the gravel makes. She
has his bucket full of ice,
silver tongs (shined daily),
his glass, his ashtray,
his celery stalks stuffed
with Roquefort cheese
on a monogrammed
platter. Soft lamplight
plays on the studded
leather chair. She banishes
me to nowhere, for it's five
o'clock, time for him
to become again
the man he isn't and
the man he is.

The Cops

After five o'clock,
father brought home
Stan Devreaux, 9th Precinct Motorcycle Squad, in jodhpurs,
and other leather-booted Suffolk County cops—
their power, their numbered badges—
to share some shots with them,
the swagger of their cursing.

Two hours into whiskey,
my name was called. I was
to be scrutinized by the men,
their caps pushed back,
sprawled against the bar.

The revolvers strapped to their hips
made me hate
my own two spindle-arms,
every pimple on my cheeks.

Father's tongue was pus-runny thick.
There were no ice-cubes in his glass.

Stamp Album

I thought I'd found the one
with the airplane
upside down—but no,
my mistake.
                    Not once
in all those years
of mounting hinges,
plate-blocks, first-day covers,

did I find among the flags
of nations and presidential faces
one small deviance
from the norm
                    so that I
might find myself.

Running Away

My mother is pressed like a garment,
no starch, hair bleached to sunshine. Dusk.
Downstairs, the day drowns drunk.

I, up here, tack my plans to my wall, run lists
of amenities, tell myself to be strong,
tell myself to not cry out as I did

when the trolley door closed on my arm
as I clutched her hand, she who ran
alongside, faster than the train's

crackling sparks, the metal
tracks, her little hat askew,
my red snowsuit soaked in sweat.

Christmas Morning

I abhorred the family
ritual. We sat on the floor
as if in mourning
to open our gifts, tearing off
the wrappings and the ribbons,
the room awash in paper heaps.

I bent down
to pick up a fallen globe,
its blue-green iridescence,
even greener, even bluer
among the ornamented boughs, full
of the room's light.
The day itself was tinsel-dust, fallen.

When I flung the sack of trash
over my shoulder, my father was
shouting *ho, ho, ho,* and mother was
taking my picture, the flash going crazy.
She'll name this one
Our Little Santa.

Into the stench of the December air,
I went outside alone, a Jew
who never learned Hebrew
as his friends had, who
wasn't called to the Torah at thirteen.

No Jewish prayers, no candles,
the festival of light snuffed by my parents.
I pushed into the garbage pail
everything I carried, and Chanukah—so much vapor
out there, gone.

Time Lines

Miss Finch taught us to draw a timeline.
Mine was ruled, a column
of soldiers moving from war to war.

My grandpa died.
I saw my father cry
beside the body. I knew enough
not to touch the corpse.
Father said, *No one will ever
do this to me again.*
At the graveside,
they lowered the body, ordered me
to throw some dirt. I obeyed.

I imagined grandpa's bones
smoothed and turned into lines
on the cold gray face of the stone,
and how the light would pick up everything
left of him.

Soft Boy

I was nursed
on formulae, that algebra
of the soft boy, all my problems
worked out in chalk on the board—
the quotient of my self
divided by myself.
I'd tuck my sex between my thighs,
to see if I could be the little girl
Mother never had.
I let that tender vein give in
to the harsh equation
of what a son should be:
a man.

Dorothy

I remember
those Valentine's Day
offerings to Mom,
Barricini Chocolates, the flowery card
taped to the heart-shaped box:
so much sentiment, its saccharine promise.

My own heart hammering
from the bike trip to *Gulkisses*—
where Dorothy, the girl with the club foot
limped and lugged the hearts
for sale (a big one open on the counter)
and the heavy cards trimmed in lace (like her blouse)
under the Hallmark sign. Me, age twelve.

For your Mom or girlfriend? she asked
as I ran my fingers over the edges
of the cellophane, clearly clinging,
like her big black shoe, laced up tight,
that rubbed her raw, twenty years or more
without a Valentine.

It's for my Mom, I said. *I don't have a girlfriend.*
Was it love itself
that prompted this admission?
Or the abundance of love words
crowding the store,
the aching sweetness of the day?

Dorothy turned unsteadily and asked,
Won't you be my Valentine?

She held me in her awkward smile,
so full, so different.
I knew only that we were alone
together in the world
where something shifted
as she handed me
my change.

College

We watched from our windows,
hidden, little more than a minion of Jews
in our new fraternity house, two weeks
into the lease.

A throng is what it was, all of them
in blue blazers, shirts buttoned down,
ties striped red and blue, each a flag,
loud, but not unruly. And we watched

the sea of blazers part and the cross rise up,
burning, while they sang *Onward Christian Soldiers*.
It was 1957, Charlottesville, home of Jefferson
and his University. We cowered there,

on Madison Lane, where the Greek elites
with names like *Deek* and *Kappa Nu*
allowed not a single Jew inside their houses.

We couldn't speak. If they had chanted, *Strip,*
would we have let them march us naked through the streets?
Would I, like so many who died before me,
have dug my own grave to stay alive a little longer?

The Beginning

Before I had a self, I grew
in the half-dark, half-light world
I knew belonged to me.

Two disappointing gods
shaped me. Before I had
a self, I was a topiary.

Birds were everywhere
in me, singing, while I
stood mute.

One day, the gods split
this world in two.
Before I had a self,

I was taken by each of them
to the great sea of disillusionment,
thrown in from separate shores.

My first-self emerged from the sea,
my body soaked in brine.
I could taste my own salts.

To be washed clean,
to be naked and alone,
to become the very brink you live on

is to bury your gods,
as your heirs will bury you.
This is genesis, where we begin.

II. Family Man

Father-Son Business

The buyer phoned.
Our prices were too high.
Get competitive, he said,
give me
three-to-five percent
by this afternoon.

Father
slammed the door,
locked us in
his office to review
my failures
as a man. He said
buyers bluff, and this one
was preying on my lack
of backbone.

Cut our prices, father said,
and the buyer
has you by the balls.

Either way, he had me
assume the eunuch's role:
my voice sacrificed
in the service of pocket change.

Magic-Form Mannequin

First time in a sales booth
at the display show with my father,
I watched him raise it
over his head and slam it
into a wall, acrylic breasts first.
I heard that body thud—
but when he held her up,
there wasn't a scratch on her: no crack, no mark,
and the buyers went wild.

Men in suits lined up to take a turn.
Some threw her
against the fire door, others
ground their heels into her chest.
None could break her.

I loved the way he smiled at me
when I smashed two forms together
and dared the toughest looking men
to beat them with their fists,
joking with the buyers
about my girlfriend's tits
being hard like these.
I felt the sweat, the heady spin
underneath the lights, the jolt
of adrenaline as I earned my place
in the company of men.

Plastic hangers

come a hundred to a carton.
The clear ones, the ones one
can see through, emit
a tone close to the brittleness
of bone. The opaque white
are muffled the way we are
in clothes.

When I shake a box,
I can tell the size: ladies,
kids, or teens, and if designed
for dresses, skirts, or suits.
I can describe their clips.
I'll know if the carton's shy
one or two—if any might be
broken. I am a hanger man.
Look what I know.

Now I trail
my fingers over their shoulders
and the surface of their bodies.
I flex their arms. That's all
I need to know if they are pure,
if they will do the work.
Were they made in too much heat?
Are they too rough? Will they break?

I am a hanger man,
                        listening.

Where I Was Going

I.
Where was I going under the weight
of my bookbag, case law, and statutes? Not to the
Harvard Café for Salisbury steak and mashed potatoes.
Not to the cinderblock dorms, their dimly lit corridors
of thought. Not home. Where was I going so full of
argument and words?

II.
I joined the cynical and jaded. My father hired me.

Not to work next to illegal aliens in the plastics factory.
Not to load forty-two-foot trailer trucks with
one hundred forty thousand garment hangers, stacked
in cases, side-by-side, front-to-back, floor-to-
ceiling, every cubic inch packed tight.

Not to the boss's office where the Harvard Law degree
vanished into *uh-oh, here comes the boss's son.*
Not to the trade shows at the Hotel New Yorker
where I licked the soles of jobbers, plied them
with booze.

III.
Where was I going? To the fertility expert with my semen
in a jar? Never to Little League with my son. Never
to go ice-skating with my daughter. Where was I going?

Not three times a week to Dr. Bernie, self-indulgent,
taking a magnifying glass to my problems. He said
I had it wrong. We were removing the magnifying glass.

IV.
Where was I going, going to
my father's funeral, my mother's grave. I was going
to the closing when I sold the business. I was going
to my daughter's wedding, to the firehouse where my son
showed me his gear and the enormous truck
he drove to Ground Zero.

Where was I going? Not to grow fables of my own
making: I was just going to my wife's studio
to help support her art. I was going to write a poem for her,
always my best reader.

The Difficulty in Making a Baby

It is said that a couple in bed
bring their parents
to the party, so here we are,
your father with a big cigar,
my father with a bottle of scotch,
your mom toting all her pills,
mine clunking along in her wheelchair,
smiling. It's hard to believe
we actually made a child like this,
distracted from lovemaking
by setting a table for them all
and rustling up some eggs and bacon,
orange juice carefully poured
into each crystal glass. Still,
we devoted ourselves to each other,
let our forebearers fend for themselves,
allowed the tumult of our bodies
to tell them off, to say get lost,
this is our time alone, and finally,
they skulked away into that theoretical
realm, found in textbooks,
that explores the many selves we are:
even when tête-à-tête,
accompanied by a high-strung quartet.

A Problem

From above a couple
of parallel lines, a diagonal
that intersects them both.
This is given. One line's mine;
the other, yours. They measure
the time we've spent together
over fifty years. If I asked, what's this
slanted line that runs right through us,
would you say fate: the brutal certainty
that cuts? Or would you see
a shaft of light, a lightning bolt?
So much mystery still cries
between us: how we've come to know
we know so little of each other.
Let's draw figures and dare to ask
what secrets they might hold. Let's be bold
for time is running short. Don't cry
about our getting old. Let's draw.
Let's talk.

You Draw Me

I love to pose for you,
be the center of your attention.
All I ask is more dimension
where I need it most. I feel
your fingers, the charcoal scratch
across my pecs, a dusting
of my buttocks, the belly, too convex.
You smile when you tell me
not to move, as if this moment
of who I am were being captured
on your pad. In your eyes,
I see myself invented, as I was in sex,
and I am still, so still, with you,
you wild-haired woman of my life.

The Swimming Pool

I always wanted a pool.
Father disapproved.
Too dangerous for your kids,
he said, sipping his drink.

So I burned five summers,
a gelding sweltering in his shadow,
before I called in the bulldozers
to level and excavate my soil.

But not before I wrote a brief.
My argument a succinct yet
humble plea, entered prostrate
as the trees began to fall.

The verdict was just, I guess.
It's your life. So sentenced,
I dug deep, moved the earth
and eventually learned to dive.
Taught my kids to do the same.

Wild Kingdom

We drive through Wild Kingdom.
Baboons present themselves.
The largest, the oldest one,
sits apart on his outcropping of rock, gazing
beyond the world. He seems indifferent
to our blue Explorer, the way his brood bounces
upon the roof. They groom themselves squatting
on the hood. I tell the kids he's the philosopher-
king. My son says he's old. My daughter
thinks he's dying. My wife is laughing
when a female ambles toward him, turns her back,
extending her pink, swollen rump, undulating,
her lips smacking, flashing teeth over her shoulder.
He mounts her. *Let's go home*, Mimi says
to the kids. *I want to read Plato with your father,*
that part about the Absolute Good. We start
to move again, toward home, past the pride of lions.
I did my best not to speed, though I wanted to.

Cycles

In their final spin,
my pair of pants, your cotton blouse
begin to blur, a single streak of color,
each lost in the other
before the cycle ends.

Let's drench ourselves
and tumble
in a storm of arms and legs
—then billowing—
touch and tangle on a line,

allowing time itself to dry us.
Stay here with me
in the slow, sweet, simultaneous heat
of our bodies, the frenzied spin
before the cycle ends.

It's Dawn

Our half-circle driveway is a smile
or a frown
depending on your point of view.
The New York Times lies
on the ground like an abandoned loaf
of bread. Overhead, crows
weave raucous circles
against the just-lit sky.
A staccato burst from them—
shrill and territorial. This time,
I cup my lips, my call a claxon
screaming to the trees, and they
chime back. I lean my paper
against the house, walk my land,
crowing.

Sandbox

His gurgling
        sounds so endearing,

pouring each grain
    on his fat oiled feet,

the toes
    he holds in his hands,

                I push
my nose between

my son's toes,
      pretend to sneeze,

tickling
    him, backs of knees,

his
    giggling squeals surge;

             I kiss
his belly,

      my beard
        my lips

          my face
pressed to him,
      father love.

Condolence Call, September 18, 2001

Dead end, that suburban street
congested with stars,
stripes, grief. We stream in,
in the weeping dark. A close-up
of his helmeted face,
pinned to the door, leaps
in candlelight that floods
the porch. Not a moth in sight.
Not a cricket or a barking dog.
The collection box,
just inside, is like a casket:
mahogany lined in silk.
Five kids, wife, an aged mother
left. His youngest daughter
takes my hand in hers,
and when I bend to kiss her cheek,
she asks me to play checkers
in her room. We sit on the floor,
pull close her sleeping dolls.
She tells me, *I want the black pieces.*
We line up all our men.
Smoke before fire, I say.

Fireman

For my son, Matthew

Two days after the towers fell,
he went in, wearing
his protective gear, leaving
me in fear of what he'd see.
But he was trained to work
in death's company.
I could never search for the dead
as he did that day.
                     He spared me
all he saw inside, his eyes
cold, the blue
of that terrifying sky.

Between

My father, my son, my bare
feet on their shoulders:
I straddle the generations.

How long can they bear me?
Do they plot my overthrow?
I don't know how I got up

here, balanced
on the brawny edge of power,
my toes curling into their flesh.

Death Notice

The day I pronounced
my son dead
I filled out no certificate.
I'm not a doctor.
Nor did I sit on a pine bench.
I'm not Orthodox.
Rather, I stood over him,
as my father stood over me,
and there, inside my wife's
walk-in closet, his mother's closet,
where he had filled his pockets
with her jewels, money she'd hidden
in several pairs of shoes,
I said it: *You're dead.*
You're dead is exactly what I said.
With lifeless eyes, he spoke—
It's about time you noticed.

Armoire

                                   In this room,
all the secrets of our lives play out
and the plot hinges
                    on the dance
between closed doors and the opening of them,
and our drawers of perfectly folded things.
No need
            to make the edges straight
and true. In the steady swing, in the soft arc,
and sharp radii, the latch, the key,
you come back to me.

Examining Room

You sit, Father,
goosebumped on the table,
gowned in paper,
weary.

You spit it out,
your left eye turning in,
No heroics.

You stand, slap your hips
with both palms
(like you always do)
playing holstered-cowboy,
your hands, index fingers
snapped out, like six-shooters.

You strike that pose
rehearsed for close to eighty years,
your white-whiskered jaw,
all of you too tough to kiss.

*I must not lose
my silhouette,* you say, your fingers
extended still until
gently I help you
with your pants.

You said no to chemo.

Now you're gone
but that moment of choice stays with me.

Trust

I buried my father's body in the earth,
dug his grave the way he told me to,
no ceremony or prayer. And though

he trusted me with his final disposition,
he placed all that remained of his possessions
in a spendthrift trust to protect me

from myself. So I live on the income
cranked from the machinery of the bank
he chose as trustee. If his trust could speak,

it would say with every monthly check,
You're not to be trusted. I deposit the money,
take in everything conveyed, my life

framed by inheritance.
I never chose his headstone,
never found

words to do him justice.

Outside My Window

In the time it took
for the squirrels
to blur themselves
into a gray play
of belly and tail,
my mother died.

I wailed
as I did when I was
newly born, now
my hand holding hers.

Groomed

I between their breaths,
caught between their teeth,
eating what they ate.

I opened ears to them:
they filled me up with words,
hers hurting, his slurred.

I mouthed no sound,
their lips
hot and cold.

I walk their steps.
I fill
their shoes.

I take their leaves.
With shovel, I
groom their graves.

Role Play

I sit in one chair
pretending to be my father.
I sit in another
pretending to be myself

at six or seven, or
a grown man wrestling
with his ghosts.

I tell my father's story
in his voice: *I was nursed*
on booze. When I was seventeen,
my kid brother's kidneys failed.
My mother told everyone:
"The good one died."

He was pissed,
that son-of-a-bitch I loved.
I, too, was deep inside
his rage and heartache.

Brine and Rosewater

For my daughter, Jennifer

I dreamed up a spool of invisible yarn
and, while she slept, I wrapped her
in gossamer and charms. They grew
as she grew. I dreamed up sweet balm
for her fingertips, that her hands
to be hands of healing. Her eyes
needed nothing more. They listen
for words that hide behind other words.

After the years doused us both
with brine and rosewater,
she said, *Daddy, I love you as I did*
when I was your little girl.
She kissed my cheek. From her
lips, a silver thread wove
itself into my beard.

I don't believe in magic,
except with her.

Wedding

My daughter sleeps in our name
but tonight she will step out
of those bedclothes.

Flowers are loaded into trucks.
Guests, like iron filings, draw
closer to the magnet.

We will gather, two by two,
and proceed as the quartet
fugues and counterpoints.

There will be a turning over,
vows: *I do* and *I will,*
dancing, arms up into the void,

a whirling gown, a fog of veil,
black-tie hurricane.
As separate as I am from sleep

so we shall be, too soon.
My daughter sleeps in her name
in another room.

The Basket of Gifts

I was given a large basket of gifts,
each one wrapped in its own unique fabric
so each felt different from the others.
And each fabric was a different color,
so each looked different from the others,
and when I lifted the gifts from the basket
I smelled their different scents, as if the colors
had their own odors, and I felt the colors
as if the colors had their own bodies, the gifts
full of mysterious wisps of sensory delight
I found in their grasping.
                       But the day came
when the basket was empty, for the gifts
had been opened and consumed over time,
rich aromas, taken by the wind,
feel of flesh, abraded by the years,
vibrant colors, erased by the fog,
only the memories of the basket were left,
and when it grew cold in my hands, my children
took the basket from me, and I pleaded with them,
to sit awhile and listen to my stories, let me tell you
about the gifts I was given in this basket,
and they listened, but they could not fathom
what I was saying. Each of them was busy
with his own basket and, when I was done speaking,
they threw away my basket, tidied up, kissed me,
and said goodbye.

Afterlife

When I return
to those who love me,
I'll have no blemishes,
not even those small scars
adolescence left.
I'll appear stripped
of poses and appliances,
dressing gowns, clowns' noses,
exaggerated frowns worn
for attention whenever I came home.
The children will find me
naked, without guile, as I
never was—and may never be again.

III. Leading Man

Shadow Life

Machines grind and blow leaves into dusty bags, hoisted
on shoulders, the gardeners gathering.
Their harvest is the trees' loss.

It takes the lake to make a line of moonlight, the moon itself
a shining example, an ample horizontal with neither left nor right,
a fading center, spent in an instant.

On the sunlit trunk of the pine, a bird's shadow flickers
like my own shadow's life cast upon those rings
of years out there in the light; in here, turned inside out.

Against a Wall

Sometimes, when the moon
is courted by wolves,
and the bats shake themselves out,

I'll move through the mouth
of the cave like a breath,
press against a windowpane,

and there inside the house
a frail young boy stands stiff
against a wall. His father measures him.

His mother, tanned, hair bleach-blonde,
shines the sterling silver tray,
then serves a fifth of Haig & Haig

in the cut crystal drinking glass.
The boy's dismissed
the minute his father takes a sip.

I've pressed my ear
to the landscaped ground
and heard the panic in his retreat

on tiptoe, in stocking feet.
His only trace, his father's mark,
indelible on the measuring wall.

Though I cannot leave
the dark until it's dark,
I do survive.

Here, inside this cave,
bats hang
harmless as handkerchiefs.

I can hear my tardy rebel stir
from years of sleep,
rising up, stretching his limbs,

hungering for light.
Soon, I will follow him out,
marking the walls as I go.

Alternatives

Sitting down to Raisin Bran in a white bowl,
banana slices starry-eyed in skim milk,
the Sunday *Times* on my gray Formica table,
I am engaged by falsehoods, the rise and fall of currencies,
critical palaver, weddings, obituaries . . .
And in this ellipsis I call *a minute or two*
the otherwise dies.

This is the real cost of what we do—each life
a blind embossing raised on a parchment of alternatives.

When I look at the moon from my favorite spot
and I review the palm trees and the phone calls from the kids,
the Judys, the Anns (girlfriends from my past),
the hot fumbling in cinder-block dorms,
and I think about the case law I ignored, the pleas
entered in three-piece suits and those on bended knees,
the way I contracted out contact with the earth,
the deep digging, how planting turns to plants, how
everything turns when left unattended, I imagine
myself a character in a book still unfinished.

Though I'm the author of fictions I call *my past*,
a brooding biographer of what might have been,
I'm still a hero on the precipice of the yet unwritten.
Oh, God, source of what I call *my time left*,
source of the possible, help me economize.

Sunsets

It's not the sunset,
but the fire-eaters
that arrest me
on the foot of Duvall Street
in old Key West.
I'm tired of sunsets,
their predictable fall
below the horizon.
I want something
hot in my mouth,
a blistering
taken in
the way my father
swallowed a fifth
each day at dusk.
Oh, what that dusking
made of him.
Those cruel sunsets,
Mother and I
like street mimes
dancing,
saying nothing.

Among the Shadows

Nights I cannot sleep, I scurry
from room to room
among the shadows, as I did

when Mother down the hall
cried out in pain and asked me
to stick her with the needles—

My son the acupuncturist,
she would say as I twirled
the steel barbs beneath her skin

and told her how I dreamt
of this when she changed
my diaper and stuck me

with a pin. How I wish
I could revise the past,
blue-pencil those cold

distances, the high horses
I mounted—my need so great
I forgot her in her quandary

quarrying for one glitter in the canyons
of her days—these rooms,
her days in them on the walls,

the bedside tables, the lamp-lit
desk at which she read Prufrock
and made her notes—daring me

to eat a peach—demanding
that I walk the beach
and breathe and listen—

let go, she said, *let go,*
rid yourself of all restraint,
you're trapped like me

in this goddamned chair—
I cannot walk, but you can
son, so walk, run, fly,

fling yourself into the world,
drink the moon, and tonight
I run from room to room,

feel the moon inside me pull,
as if arms were pulling me
in two. I'm thrown between them

once again, my father
the captain, my mother the crew,
and me, the stowaway

along for the ride, without
a life boat, a jacket,
or a place to hide from the furious

storm, these moon-crazed waves,
this squid-ink sky. We're in the drink.
Our ship splits apart.

Mother drifts away—I cling to him.
He makes for shore. *Stop your clinging!*
he says. And I do.

Broken Promises Made at Age Six

Promise me,
he said,
when I'm in
the hospital, you'll
sneak a bottle
in the bed with me.

Promise me,
he said,
when I am
dead, you'll
put a bottle
in the box with me.

Promise me,
he said,
you'll
leave unsaid
these promises
you've made to me.

Because I wouldn't
keep my word,
father turns
in his dry grave,
and I write
it all down.

Preparing Breakfast

I lose myself in the slow peeling
of my morning banana, the bed
of bran flakes waiting for each
disc to fall from the small red
knife, every starry-eyed slice
some kind of miracle. Zen
in the art of blueberry sprinkling,
not thinking when the ripe
peach yields its juice to steel.
I swear I can see the origins
of life in the pit, its surrounding
flesh, and in milk spilt to the bowl
with the articulation of my wrist.
On the surface of the spoon, my
distorted face rested, before I ate,
lifting it to my waiting lips.

The Idea

Every few weeks they take my blood
of no value now to anyone. Today,
two chemo patients hooked to drips
turn pages of *Vanity Fair* and *Business Week*.
Sarah has no hair and Bill is pale as chalk.
We three sit in padded barber chairs, feet up.
I ask Sarah, *What're you here for?*
The laughs, she says. I say, *I'd do my stand-up act,*
but . . . and she cracks up. Then Bill chimes in
with a question: *Is there an afterlife? Yes,* I say,
though in your case it might not be a blessing.
Why not? Bill asks. *Because you're coming back*
as a lawyer. Bill looks skeptical. *How do you know?*
God, of course, I reply. *He calls me every day*
to thank me for my blood. He said he uses it
to paint sunsets and autumn leaves. Bill says,
That's a nice idea. Sarah shouts across the room,
Did God happen to mention what he did with my tits?
Sarah darling, I said, *He told me He worships*
the idea of your breasts. Same here, Sarah said.
Same here, Bill said. Then we said it together, *Same here.*

Role Play

I am the mother of everything
begun but never finished.
This time the father isn't overthrown.
This time, I do not play the son.

Future folds itself upon its dotted lines.
Each day, we are ushered in.
Each day, we bolt for the exit door
while the air grows thin as an atrophied limb.

There's whispering. This one coughs.
I've grown weary of the starry map above
and wary of its promised fixity.
Suffering wears me like a pumice stone.

We return to where the film began.
I hold Achilles' ankle in my hand.

A Portrait on the Day It Hit Home

He had pressed his body weight
in eight six-rep sets then run
three seven-minute miles
around the reservoir,
cooled down, walking
the path out of the park,
and stretched facing North on Fifth
where his parents had lived
before they split into
divorced people,
shattering him just a bit,
disordering him enough
to require a fresh shirt and tie,
a rigid diet and vanity plates
I 4 AN I,
when it hit him, the news
of his death, it hit
home and he owned it
slightly out of breath,
almost forgetting
his doorman's name
to whom he'd said good morning
every morning
for over fifteen years,
Good morning, F-frank,
just that slight faltering
before he took to the stairs
stopping on the first landing
hands on his knees
crouching, then straightening up,
and entering the hall
he had never entered before
taking the elevator up
to his own floor

where the morning paper rested
against his door,
and he knew the climb
was now too much for him,
as he pressed his thumb
against the glass
his unique print reviewed
allowing him to pass
into his plush uncertain future.

First Visit to My Father's Grave
Ten Years After His Death

A decade gone, each hour, a death
of sorts. And just today I thought
about the Lionel train you brought
home to me, no liquor on your breath.

You made a circle of three-rail track,
but left each piece an inch apart,
then taught, *male into female*, the art
of coupling, lost on me. I lacked

connectedness with you. But then,
you pinned a medal on my chest,
a purple heart. *You are the best,*
you said. I don't remember when

the purple heart and wounded in the war
came together. But here, at your grave,
a lifetime later, it's time we forgave
each other, old wounds, ancient scores.

Breakfast Nook

Too many daffodils, every face
cowardly and furious
like school kids at Columbine.
So cruel, their nodding,
their fragile stands, their complicity
with whisps of forsythia and open-
mouthed tulips. Nothing so random
as our garden's indifference,
unattended, out of control.

On the radio, troops are killing,
killed. Between our crusade
and their jihad, is there a way
to divinity?
                The coffee brews.
I peel away the orange rind.
Even now, Jerusalem is sliced
in two.

To the Poets

I have lined up my servants on book shelves.
I work for them. They serve me well.
They welcome me in quiet, in tumult,
even in death's company. They humble me.
They make me in their imagery. I am
their papier-mâché. Their hands are all
over me, as I reach out to them. I steal
their songs. I am a felon on parole.
They gave me life. They have pardoned me.

Odyssey

I stayed out of my inner life this fall,
turned my eyes to the trees,
walked and walked under oak/maple/beech
to see the last leaf fall. I watched the wind
do its work, its toothless saw shivering
in raw increments.
I wanted to find the end,
to cross the line
desire crossed to hibernate.
But that's a fiction.
There's always a leaf left unscathed,
a flash of orange
in the chiseled blue of winter.
I am as restless as the seasons.

My Passing

Unseen, the kumquats
ripen, so too the grass,
its lengthening
and its falling back.

I have yet to choose
a final resting place.
Beside my mother,
or by my father?

They are buried
in separate plots
as they always were.
It's hard to choose

between them,
as it always was.
I have bones to pick
with both of them.

Perhaps my body
should give itself
to fire, ashes
taken by the wind.

I know there will be
a tomorrow with
no tomorrows.
All my yesterdays

bequeathed
to my family
as memories.
They too shall pass.

We Go to Bed Again

Just before I stuff another day
into the envelope of night,
I hesitate as if my takes
and double-takes could slow things down.

I imagine my old, cold feet turning
blue between the icy sheets,
how you'll *ooo* and *ooo*
should my toe so much as graze your shin.

Could giving blood a week ago
have chilled me so? My shivers shake
the walls and I feel my balls gather
in search of heat. I cannot speak.

You make a breeze lifting up the sheet.
I groan and press against your fire.
You perspire, say I'm like a corpse.
I never argue when you're right.

You get up to fetch me socks
and grandma's quilt. In the dark,
you hold my hand, whispering
my name. On your lips, I hear
myself and find myself, warming.

Love Poem for Mimi

Make me your ladder.
Wake me to myself.
Let's take liberties with each other,
delicious liberties that bind us.

The years unhidden between us,
you are me, you are my life,
each to the other completely.

Your flash of feathers, how you call,
I want the bird that's you, your sudden song.

Given

Given the drift of the ice
and the draft on the backs of our necks.

Given our knowledge
and ignorance of death.

Given the sparks that fly from the anvil,
and the smell of fish in the harbor.

Given the timid folks
gazing through their windows.

Given the bold strokes on the canvas,
the sad sounds of the hollow oboe.

Given the thumb in opposition,
the crenellated brain.

Given what we call *this* and what we call *that,*
the innate and what we make of the luck of the draw.

Given it all:

    Will we gather our shawls about our shoulders and weep?
    Will we be exiles in bedclothes and robes?
    Will we shrivel all we've been given?
    Will we allow the bank to foreclose on our children?

Right here, right now, the sea
is lit by the moon. We are given
phosphors and low-flying birds.

Given the stars,
why must we constellate the sky?

Night writes its journal in black ink.

Directions

There are no signs or markers—
no signals here. You'll have to listen
to find your way. Don't leave
in fog, or when the clouds white out
the light of day. You'll need
the early morning sun to stretch
the shadow of the tallest pine
which you must follow as it climbs
the gentle slope, covered now with cones,
and when the grade grows steep
and your breathing deepens, stop.
Rest awhile by the stones that sit
like hours on the face of a clock.
What better place to find your way
than alone in a circle of silence?

Later, on the crest,
you'll share the sky with eagles
where the wind touches every weed
and carries every seed
to greening.

From the far side,
you'll see the city bubbling below,
the ribboning of chimney smoke.
It's a slow descent to the marketplace.
Take time to look around
at the sound of scrubgrass,
the layered smells of shale, the taste of quartz.

Carry a stick as you walk down,
or gather a bunch of wild flowers.
Hold onto something
from the summit
so you can find your way
back up again.

A Room of Approximations

It's daybreak: white sky, early chill,
the lake, pines and birches still,
like the frogs and birds. There's a line
where the sky and timber meet
to define the world; yet in the lake,
I can't divine trees from sky.
The morning mist clings
and steals details from the surface.

If I walk down to the vague reeds,
to the muffled sounds of frogs,
immerse my feet in the minnowed edge of things,
I'd still not see beyond my limited periphery.

How does the mist, now tiny puffs, move
and the trees remain motionless?
Could the leaves seek the breeze
as the heron hunts the fish?
Might this mist be composed of clouds

mirrored in the lake's surface?
Maybe, I have it wrong.

How little of this world I know.

Miles A. Coon resides in Palm Beach, Florida, with Mimi, his wife of more than fifty years. He received an M.F.A. in Poetry from Sarah Lawrence College in 2002 after having spent thirty years in a manufacturing business. He is a graduate of Harvard Law School, class of 1962, and the University of Virginia, with highest honors, class of 1959, where he studied Philosophy and Economics. His poems have appeared widely, and his chapbook, *Homeland Security*, was published by Jeanne Duval Editions in 2005. Miles is a supporter of many non-profit poetry organizations and independent presses. He is a self-described "workshop junkie," having participated in well over fifty of them. Miles founded the Palm Beach Poetry Festival in 2005 and served as its President and Chairman of the Board until 2022.